Way to Be!

Manners on the Playground

by **Carrie Finn**   illustrated by **Chris Lensch**

PICTURE WINDOW BOOKS
Minneapolis, Minnesota

Special thanks to our advisers for their expertise:

Kay Augustine, Associate Director
Institute for Character Development at Drake University

Susan Kesselring, M.A., Literacy Educator
Rosemount–Apple Valley–Eagan (Minnesota) School District

Editor: Nick Healy
Designer: Tracy Davies
Page Production: Angela Kilmer
Art Director: Nathan Gassman
Associate Managing Editor: Christianne Jones
The illustrations in this book were created digitally.

Picture Window Books
151 Good Counsel Dr.
P.O. Box 669
Mankato, MN 56002-0669s
877-845-8392
www.picturewindowbooks.com

Printed in the United States of America.

 All books published by Picture Window Books
are manufactured with paper containing at least
10 percent post-consumer waste.

Library of Congress Cataloging-in-Publication Data
Finn, Carrie.
Manners on the playground / by Carrie Finn ; illustrated
by Chris Lensch.
p. cm. — (Way to be!)
Includes bibliographical references and index.
ISBN: 978-1-4048-3154-4 (library binding)
ISBN: 978-1-4048-3559-7 (paperback)
1. Etiquette for children and teenagers—Juvenile
literature. 2. Playgrounds—Juvenile literature.
I. Lensch, Chris. II. Title.
BJ1857.C5F48 2007
395.5—dc22   2006027566

The playground is for everyone. It is a place where people go to have fun. Good manners allow everyone to have a turn. They also help people play safely.

There are lots of ways you can use good manners on the playground.

Elliot waits his turn to ride the swing.

He is using good manners.

Beth says "Thank you!" when her friend helps her to the top of the jungle gym.

She is using good manners.

Jacob and Tim listen while the teacher explains the rules of tetherball.

They are using good manners.

There is only one teeter-totter on the playground. Still, Jessie and Melissa let their friends go first.

They are using good manners.

Cody says "Good game!" to players on the other team after they win the kickball game.

He is using good manners.

Juan says "Please" when he asks to use Kelly's jump rope.

He is using good manners.

Kim helps Jenny get up after she falls down during the soccer game.

She is using good manners.

At recess, kids fill the playground. Liam says "Excuse me" when he accidentally bumps someone.

He is using good manners.

After recess, Cheryl and Riley pick up soccer balls, baseballs, a bat, and other toys.

They are using good manners.

21

It's important to have fun and to use good manners when you visit the playground. By using good manners, everyone will get a turn, and everyone can play safely.

Fun Facts

In Colombia, lots of kids enjoy playing horseshoes.

In Afghanistan, kids like to play with kites and have kite duels.

Long ago, British soldiers used hopscotch to improve their footwork. Hopscotch is now a popular game on many playgrounds.

In Tibet, people like to watch yak racing.

In double Dutch, two people swing two jump ropes in opposite directions while one or more people jump.

A physical education teacher named James Naismith invented the game of basketball in 1891.

To Learn More

At the Library

Candell, Arianna. *Mind Your Manners: At the Park.* Hauppauge, N.Y.: Barron's, 2005.

DeGezelle, Terri. *Manners on the Playground.* Mankato, Minn.: Capstone Press, 2005.

Meiners, Cheri J. *Share and Take Turns.* Minneapolis: Free Spirit Publishing, 2003.

On the Web

FactHound offers a safe, fun way to find Web sites related to this book.
All of the sites on FactHound have been researched by our staff.

1. Visit *www.facthound.com*

2. Type in this special code: 1404831541

3. Click on the FETCH IT button.

Your trusty FactHound will fetch the best sites for you!

Index

Look for all of the books in the Way to Be! series:

Being a Good Citizen: A Book About Citizenship

Being Fair: A Book About Fairness

Being Respectful: A Book About Respectfulness

Being Responsible: A Book About Responsibility

Being Trustworthy: A Book About Trustworthiness

Caring: A Book About Caring

Manners at School

Manners at the Table

Manners in Public

Manners in the Library

Manners on the Playground

Manners on the Telephone

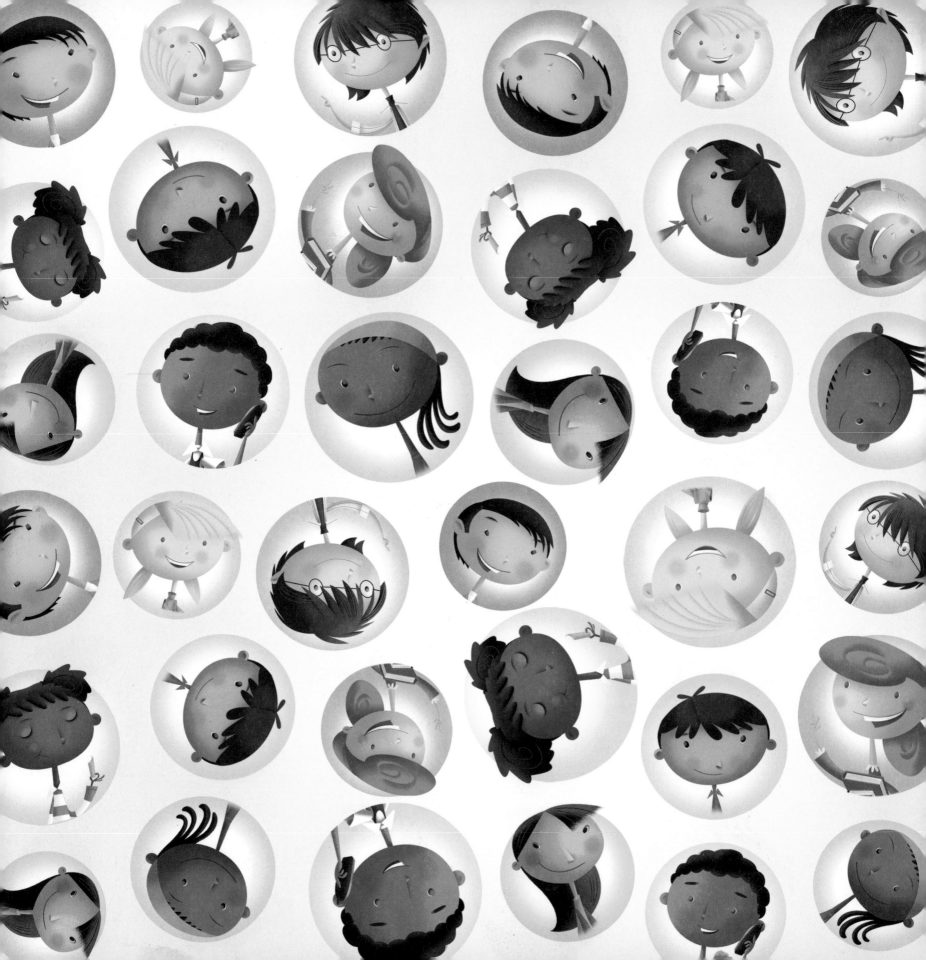